Anonymus

Vineland

Statement presented to the Jury of the Paris Exposition, 1867

Anonymus

Vineland
Statement presented to the Jury of the Paris Exposition, 1867

ISBN/EAN: 9783743310988

Manufactured in Europe, USA, Canada, Australia, Japa

Cover: Foto ©ninafisch / pixelio.de

Manufactured and distributed by brebook publishing software
(www.brebook.com)

Anonymus

Vineland

VINELAND.

....

STATEMENT PRESENTED TO THE

Jury of the Paris Exposition,

1867.

E. C. MARKLEY & SON, Printers, 422 Library Street, Philadelphia, Pa.

I hereby present my application for the Grand Prize of ONE HUNDRED THOUSAND FRANCS, *or such other prize or prizes, as you may consider me entitled to, of those constituting the Distinct Order of Reward, "instituted in favor of Persons, Establishments, or Locali= ties, which, by a Special Organization, or Special Institutions, have developed a spirit of harmony among all those co=operating in the same work, and have provided for the Material, Moral, and Intellectual well=being of the Workman."*

CHARLES K. LANDIS.

March 6th, 1867.

TO THE INTERNATIONAL JURY

PARIS EXPOSITION.

GENTLEMEN:—In presenting a statement of my enterprise whilst I claim all the benefit to the industrial population and welfare of humanity, to which it is entitled, I prefer leaving the subject more to what can be seen from the actual results produced, and the evidence of others than to anything. I will say for myself, I prefer to confine my own remarks to the bare elucidation of the principles upon which my enterprise is founded and carried out.

In the year 1861, I commenced purchasing land, and by 1865 had succeeded in purchasing about 28,000 acres, or about forty-five square miles of land.

I commenced operations in the way of public improvements,—the opening of roads, and the bringing of colonists in November, 1861. At that time the country was a dense wilderness of forest trees and thick under-growth, but with a clay and sandy loam soil, well adapted to the cultivation of fruits and the cereals. Within the wide bounds of my purchase, I do not think that there was living more than a half-dozen families. You could wander in any direction for days without meeting a human creature, and a silence reigned of that peculiar kind of which the ear is only sensible in a dense wilderness.

In founding the colony, which I have called "VINELAND," I carefully considered the principles of general policy, which would most increase the *material prosperity,* and *moral welfare* of the colonists, which would also insure a *dense* population, and produce from that population the greatest amount of industry and the highest order of intellectual improvement. Therefore, to do this, I paid the strictest attention to details in laying out the plans of the tract of land; making provision to secure its improvement and introducing the best systems of agriculture and horticulture; also to the development of the manufacturing and mercantile interests of the place and the moral good of the people, by organizing societies of learning of the best educational institutions, and the adoption of a new temperance reform, sustained by public opinion.

PRINCIPLES OF VINELAND.

I.—That the country should be laid out with a reference to practical convenience and economy or profit.

II.—That the place should be laid out with a reference to the beautiful, I, therefore, adopted my shade-tree system, provided for the grassing of the road-sides and the setting the houses back, sufficiently far, to afford room for flowers and shrubbery.

III.—To promote the physical prosperity and mental improvement and happiness of the people in the highest degree, by the development of industry, the enforcing of temperance, the formation of societies for the entertainment and improvement of the mind.

It was necessary to insure the prosperity of the colonists, as in the first years of the colony it would be composed of people of small means or entirely dependent upon their labor.

In order to insure mental improvement, it was necessary to adopt a system which would insure a population sufficiently dense to enable them to form various societies for mutual improvement, and also by reason of mutual improvement to appreciate the value of their property, as well as to form sufficient population to organize churches, schools and other societies. In order to obtain population sufficiently numerous to the square mile, I selected a market, climate and soil, the best calculated for the raising of fruit and those products most demanded in the markets of New York and Philadelphia. I introduced the best and most approved system of agriculture and horticulture. The laws in regard to fencing I had changed, and the necessity of fencing was done away with.

The country was laid out upon a general system of small farms, with parks or squares, provided for public recreation. The manufacturing and commercial interests of the place were also provided for; with this view a village plot was laid out in the centre of the tract, of about one mile square.

IV.—The lands and town lots were sold to actual colonists only. The strictest provisions were made to exclude the speculator, that *curse of new colonies in America*. No land was sold to any one for mere investment, but certain improvements had to be made within a given time or the property reverted back into my hands, to be sold again to some one who would colonize upon it. Up to January first, 1867, the money was refunded upon land that was not improved within the time specified; to that time more than $57,000 was refunded. This was not legally required, excepting in a few cases under special agreement, but was done in order to prevent distress.

The improvement system was adopted to insure the continued growth and prosperity of the colony, to promote industry, to discourage unthrifty people from purchasing, and to appreciate the value of property in the hands of the actual colonist.

In case an actual settler was imprudent in his disbursements, by reason of this appreciation, he could always sell his property, or a part of it, after his improvements were made. There was then some person with capital always ready to take his place, and he, profiting by experience, could purchase another place on the outside margin of improvement and have more capital, with which to make his improvements.

In order to carry out the above designs, agricultural, horticultural, literary and musical societies were formed, also church societies and schools of which statements will be appended.

The citizens were stimulated to exertion by various premiums for merit which were offered them. The full particulars of which will be found in the statements annexed and evidence offered.

The leading features of the colony may be presented, as follows :

MATERIAL ELEMENTS.

1. The general plan of laying out the land and by which peculiar facilities were afforded to poor and industrious people to obtain land for homesteads. To accomplish this, it was laid out in five, ten and twenty acre lots at a small price, payable in one, two, three and four years.

2. The requirements that the houses in the town plot be set back from the road-side at least twenty feet, and on the farm lots at least seventy-five feet, in order to afford room for flowers and shrubbery.

3. Requiring all colonists to plant shade trees upon the road-side and to grass the road-sides.

4. Requiring colonists to build and settle upon their lands within one year, and selling no land to other than actual colonists.

5. The introduction of fruit growing and the general improvement of agriculture and horticulture.

6. The introduction of American manufactures.

7. The making of roads and other improvements at my individual expense.

MORAL ELEMENTS.

1. The introduction of good and convenient schools.

2. The formation of agricultural and horticultural societies.

3. The formation of church societies, for the encouragement of morality and religion.

4. The formation of literary societies and libraries.

5. The introduction of a new temperance reform, which, in its practical operation, appears to do away with all the evils of intemperance.

By the advice of many friends, but with much hesitation, I am encouraged to claim that this is the first colony, where the above principles of general policy have been adopted and successfully carried out by the efforts of a single individual founder of any colony in modern times, independent of State power, and that it has done enough for the general welfare of industrious people to entitle it to the moderate consideration of the Honorable Jury.

I also beg leave to state that all information concerning my peculiar views or the principles upon which I founded the colony of Vineland, which appear in the annexed statement, and the reasons for the same were furnished by myself. I prefer that the confirmation should come in the form presented in the annexed statement, as it is embarrassing to any one to speak too much of himself.

Most respectfully,

Your obedient servant,

CHAS. K. LANDIS.

Vineland, *March 6th*, 1867.

PARIS EXPOSITION.

———————————————

GENTLEMEN :—Mr. Charles K. Landis, who is the respected Founder of the Colony of Vineland, and one of our most esteemed fellow-citizens, having announced himself to you as a competitor for one or more of the prizes designated in his Memorial, to which this paper is appended, it affords us great pleasure, in accordance with his request, to present for your consideration the following Statement of what we know in regard to his plans, the difficulties overcome, and his success.

We are all now, and have been almost from its commencement, citizens of this Colony or acquainted with its progress. From an early period in its history, many circumstances have conspired to render us familiar with the *plans* of its Founder. We have watched its development always with interest, and sometimes with *anxiety*, lest the fate so commonly attending schemes of colonization, originating in private enterprise, might overtake this movement, and leave us all a prey to disappointment and blighted hopes. Our *fears* have not been realized, but our most sanguine *hopes* have been fulfilled.

2

In our opinion, the claim of Mr. Landis to the favorable regard to the Jury, rests upon three distinct considerations.

I.—The Objects which he aimed to accomplish, especially in the *material* and *moral* welfare of industrious people.

II.—The Obstacles which had to be overcome.

III.—The Results which have been attained in successfully accomplishing the objects.

We desire, Gentlemen, to present our statement of facts in the order above proposed.

I.—The *Objects* which he proposed to accomplish.

1.—The first and leading object was, to promote *the material and moral welfare of industrious people of small means* by adopting such a policy in the affairs of the Colony as would enable such persons to obtain independent homes, and to educate their children.

This end it was believed could be attained by selling the land at a moderate price, and on a long credit, and by securing to the purchaser the full benefit of the rise in the value of real estate caused by the increase of population; for, should he be unfortunate, or miscalculate either his means or his expenses, so as to be unable to pay for the property first purchased, he could easily sell it, as improved property, at such an advance in price as would enable him to begin anew, with increased means, and an almost certain prospect of success.

In consequence of the very stringent stipulations, by which each colonist bound himself to improve his land, to which we refer more at length below, there was a moral certainty that every piece of improved land would be worth, and would actually bring in the market, much more than it had cost. As a consequence, we could mention many cases which have come within our own knowledge, in which improved property has been sold at prices ranging from one to ten times its entire cost.

2.—To bring a large tract of wild land under a high state of cultivation, to change a wilderness to fields and gardens, abounding in food for man and beast.

3.—To lay out the land in the new Colony on a plan not only consistent with order and good taste, but which should render the whole, when developed, a *model* of rural beauty. This design is best illustrated by a description of the plan actually adopted in the laying out of Vineland. A railroad runs through the Colony from north to south, on each side of which is a street one hundred feet wide. Parallel with this, at convenient distances, and also at right angles to these, are other streets or roads from fifty to one hundred feet in width. A village about one mile square, with streets from sixty-six to one hundred feet wide, is located on each side of the railroad, near the centre of the Colony. A Public Park, containing forty acres, principally covered with dense forest, is located north of the village and east of the railroad, while smaller parks and public squares are scattered here and there. Shade-trees are required to be planted at suitable distances along the streets and roads, two rows being required on each side of the wider streets or avenues. The fronts of all buildings are required to be set, in the village, at least twenty feet, and in the country at least seventy-five feet from the sides of the streets, while the road-sides are invariably to be seeded to grass, and kept in that condition perpetually by the proprietors of the adjacent lands. Such is a brief summary of those "lines of beauty" which it was proposed to trace upon the virgin soil of Vineland.

4.—To provide in the new Colony against that common curse of new countries, particularly in America, *speculation in wild lands.* No land should be sold to any person who would not come under legal obligations to improve the same, by cultivation of at least a portion of the land, and erecting a dwelling-house thereon, within a specified time from the date of purchase. On all farms sold, at least two-and-a-half acres must be put under cultivation within one year. Bonds should also be given for the planting of shade-trees, and the grassing of the road-sides within a time specified for each. No deed should be given for any property till all the improvements above recited had been made by the purchaser; or if a deed should be given, bonds should be taken for the making of these improvements. If the purchaser failed to make the improvements according to his Bond of Agreement, the land should revert to Mr. Landis, to be re-sold to another person, under the same or similar improvement stipulations.

However, though Mr. Landis has forfeited many contracts in consequence of the non-fulfilment of improvement stipulations, still he has always discriminated in favor of those who, from sickness or other unforseen accidents, may have failed to meet their engagements. In such cases he has been in the habit of refunding, not only the money paid on the contract, but in addition, the full value of whatever improvements had been made. In the year 1865 he refunded in this way more than thirty two thousand dollars, and in the year 1866 more than twenty-five thousand dollars.

Such were the means by which it was proposed to protect the colonists against the chilling influence of speculation without improvement, and at the same time *to enable them, by mutual industry, to appreciate the value of each other's property.*

5.—To relieve the colonists from the burdensome requirement of fencing their lands, and to encourage the soiling of cattle. This would require, wherever the Colony might be located, special legislation, inasmuch as there were at that time, no localities in the United States, so far as is known to us, where domestic animals were not allowed to run at large, and pasture on the public highways.

6.—To protect the colonists from the baneful effects resulting from the traffic of intoxicating liquors. This, too, would require special legislation, in order to *prevent* an evil which it has been found almost impossible to eradicate when once established. To this end, it was proposed to introduce a practical prohibition of this traffic into the *organic law* of the new Colony.

7.—To secure to the colonists the benefit of schools and other social institutions of the highest order.

By introducing fruit-culture mainly, and thus practically confining each colonist to a comparatively small piece of land, and securing a dense population, this result, it was hoped, might be obtained.

8.—To promote the health of the colonists not only by regular gymnastic exercises, but by encouraging persons of former sedentary habits, to work and live more in the open air. It was noticed that in most localities in the United States, public opinion would not tolerate women, and especially ladies of education and refinement, in any kind of out-door labor. Consequently American women are becoming physically inferior to those of other countries.

It was hoped that in this colony, a public opinion might be created, that would be less exacting and more reasonable in this respect. Hence the culture of fruits and flowers, was to be recommended to ladies, as especially adapted to their physical wants and capacities.

9.—To promote the material and moral welfare of the colonists, by enlarging their knowledge of the kindred sciences of Agriculture and Horticulture. To this end, societies were to be organized, in different parts of the colony, that should meet at stated times for the exhibition of agricultural and horticultural productions, for the mutual interchange of views on suitable questions, and for rendering mutual assistance in procuring the best and purest seeds, and the most profitable fertilizers. Premiums were also to be offered for the best productions of various kinds, with a view to stimulate a generous rivalry.

10.—Religious Institutions for the special amelioration of the moral condition of the colonists, were to be founded and encouraged. No preference was to be given to any particular denomination of Christians, in the sale of lands, nor were any of good moral character, to be excluded or frowned upon, because of anything distasteful in their religious views or practices. The Proprietor would donate lots to any religious society, that would agree to erect a church thereon. Sunday schools and kindred institutions should be encouraged, and in short all reasonable facilities should be afforded to the *good* of every creed, to exert their highest moral influence for the elevation of those who might be, in a moral sense, their inferiors.

11.—To introduce Manufactures, suitable to the tastes and circumstances of the colonists. This was not to be the first thing attempted. Farms and gardens were to be opened up and improved, as an end more important, and, at the same time, more difficult to accomplish. Afterwards, manufactures were to be established, in order to furnish a home market for fruits and farm products, as well as to accommodate those mechanics and artisans, who might be attracted to the colony by the beauty of the country, the salubriousness of the climate, the proximity to good markets, and the excellence of the schools, and other social institutions.

We are assured by Mr. Landis, that he has still other, and if possible, higher *aims* in view. But as there has not been time, even for the partial development of these further plans, we forbear, mentioning them for the present.

We beg leave to state that the above statement of principles and reasons for the same, have been received direct from Mr. Landis', and that we have experienced the results of their natural operations in our every day life in Vineland.

To keep out of the place, the sale of malt, vinous and alcoholic drinks was decided upon by Mr. Landis as an economic as well as benevolent measure. The reasons assigned at different times by him may be mentioned as follows:—

Temperance is more peculiarly necessary in a new colony than any other place.

Colonists leaving old associations and friends are less subject to restraints, and not having the resources of old friendships and amusements, the temptation to indulge amongst new acquaintances formed would be very great. When a new introduction would take place, it would be followed by a drink of fiery alcohol. When a small bargain was made at the store or market it would be followed by a drink. It is believed that three times the amount of liquor would be drank, than in an old place, to the ruin of health and resources. This is the general experience in new colonies. The colonist who would come with a very small sum of money and a family of children would find his money soon gone and his health impaired, whereas if he had remained temperate the benefit of his means and his industry would have been applied to his land, affording him a living and an independence.

In America where groggeries exist, the young men make them a place of resort, to find acquaintances and amusements, thereby ruining their health, their morals and understandings, and unfitting them for society—yet their superabundant vitality must find an outlet in some direction. In order to supply this want, Musical, Literary, Gymnastic, Elocutionary and Dramatic Societies have been organized. These societies to a great extent are sustained by the youth of both sexes, and the superabundant vitality which in one case if perverted would send them to destruction, is directed and made to serve as an active energy in their mental and physical improvement.

The effect of this is a remarkable feature in Vineland. Entertainments improving to the mind are constantly going on, and are followed as amusements, and this affords a feature which is a striking contrast to other places of equal size, but filled with groggeries, and where such entertainments would not be attractive.

II.—The *Obstacles* which had to be overcome.

1.—The selection of a suitable *location*. It must be in a healthy region; it must be in a mild climate; the land must be cheap; it must be convenient to good markets; it must be signally adapted to the growth of fruits, especially small fruits, such as strawberries, raspberries, blackberries, grapes and dwarf pears. To find such a location was no easy task. The great Mississippi Valley was thoroughly canvassed. Some locations were found to be good for fruit, but the climate was found to be unhealthy, or the markets inconveniently distant. Others were fruitful and well situated, but the prices of land were beyond the reach of any but the wealthy class. Finally, the Tract now called Vineland, in Southern New Jersey, was selected, as possessing in the highest degree, a happy combination of the most desirable and necessary points.

2.—The location once fixed, it was necessary to turn the tide of emigration in that direction. Vineland was indeed situated upon a railroad : but that railroad was in no sense a thoroughfare. Crowds of emigrants of various nationalities, thronged all the thoroughfares leading *Westward* from the Atlantic cities; but scarce any one, American or foreigner, thought of migrating to Southern New Jersey. Had the new colony been located in Illinois or Minnesota, nothing would have been needed, but simply to arrest the emigrant wave, while sweeping past the desired point. But no such wave was sweeping over Vineland. There the social waters were still, even to stagnation, and it seemed as if it would require an angel's effort to trouble them.

3.—Prejudices of the strongest kind had to be removed. True, every one admitted that the climate of Vineland was both healthful and agreeable. Its proximity to the best markets in America could not be denied; it was only thirty-four miles from Philadelphia, and one hundred and twenty-five from New York. But the soil—what of that? Ask Rumor, and she will tell you that Southern New Jersey is nothing but a heap of drifting white sand. Are there not good farms in some localities—in Salem, Cumberland, Atlantic and Cape May Counties? "Oh, yes," says Rumor, "but these localities are completely isolated—nothing but *oäses* in the midst of a barren desert." Ask the native Jerseyman, living in the vicinity of Vineland, and he will tell you, that these Vineland lands are good for nothing but to raise cord-wood, to supply the furnaces of the Glass-works; that they will never pay, by cultivation, for the expense of clearing them. When it became publicly known that Mr. Landis was about to found a colony in New Jersey, there were not wanting those who conceived it to be their *duty* to write let-ters to the leading Agricultural journals of the Northern States, warning the people against throwing away their time and money in visiting Vineland and purchasing lands there. The consequence was, that when any one spoke of going to Vineland, the common remark was: "What! going to Vine-land! Going to settle on a Jersey sand-bank! Be careful, or you will wake up some morning and find your house buried in a sand drift!" These misrepresentations were the more injurious, in that they were made by persons who were supposed to know all about the matter, and who had a good reputation for honesty.

In regard to the quality of the Vineland soil, the fact is, that it is by no means too sandy to be productive, but on the contrary, contains an abundance of alumini, and is highly fertile. The roads in their natural state, are generally hard and good, which is never the case where the land is very sandy. Why then did the rumor as to its sandy character ever gain circulation or receive credence? Simply because there are in Southern New Jersey tracts of sandy land, which are generally known, and with which this extensive tract has been confounded. By persistent efforts in disabusing the pub-lic mind, this prejudice against Vineland soil has been in a great measure removed, but much time and labor were required to compass this result.

4.—The absence of all those natural features, which con-stitute elements of success in new countries, was in a nega-tive sense, an *obstacle* of no small magnitude. Vineland has absolutely nothing besides its climate, its soil, and its proximity to good markets, to recommend it to the colonist or the capitalist. It has neither *water-power*, nor *coal*, nor *iron*, nor *vast stores of timber for lumbering purposes*, nor even a *faint suspicion of petroleum*. Even the deposit of *marl*, which render other portions of New Jersey rich, are not known to exist in Vineland. In short, there are here *no special facilities or appliances for money-making;* and whatever material prosperity this colony enjoys above other portions of Southern New Jersey, is due to the *wisdom* and *creative energy* of its Founder, seconded by the *industry* and *good conduct* of the colonists. We are even destitute of what so many of the towns of this Peninsula enjoy, namely, communication by water with Philadelphia and New York. All our surplus produce must go to market by the railroad, and we have not even a competing line of road to keep down the prices of transportation. This lack will undoubtedly be remedied in time, but it has thus far been a serious annoyance.

5.—The constant efforts of speculators to evade the improvement stipulations, formed a serious obstacle. No matter how firmly bound to make certain improvements within a specified time, the speculator would endeavor, by coaxing, by making excuses, by asking for extensions of time, or even by threats of litigation, to hold the land from year to year, without improvement, knowing that he could then sell it at a great advance. Had the importunities of such men been heeded, a large proportion of the new colony would have been at this moment unimproved, which is now under a high state of cultivation. On several occasions, within the last three years, interested parties, for their own selfish ends, have endeavored to thwart Mr. Landis in his business, and to break down the established policy of the colony. These endeavors were the more injurious, from the fact, that the Vineland enterprise was and is a *purely private one.* Mr. Landis has never asked for or obtained any *special legislative protection*, any *chartered privileges*, or any *monopoly* of any kind. In the absence of any law of the State, to protect the infant colony from the intrusion of evil-minded persons, who might do incalculable injury, either by establishing opposition land-offices, by forming secret cabals, or by fomenting disaffection in the minds of the colonists; the only means by which such protection could be secured, was *by bringing the force of an overwhelming public opinion to bear upon all such schemes, and frowning them down.*

Such an occasion arose about one year ago, when an open and flagrant attempt was made to establish a rival land-office in Vineland, for the purpose of sending the visitors away, who came by the efforts of Mr. Landis, and induce them to purchase in other sections and States, and in other ways to cripple Mr. Landis in his efforts to develop the resources of the colony. A mass meeting of the citizens was called, speeches were made, resolutions were adopted, and the Report of the Committee previously appointed, embodying the main feature of the " Vineland Policy," after a full and free discussion, was adopted by acclamation, the vote being almost unanimous. There were supposed to be about *two thousand male citizens* present, and we have rarely witnessed a more enthusiastic gathering of the people. The result was, that the obnoxious land-office, was closed a few days afterwards, without any disturbance or violation of the law.

6. The efforts, almost constant, of various enemies of the colony, to turn away strangers while on the way to Vineland, has been one of the most serious obstacles. These persons have been, generally, agents and runners for various land offices in Philadelphia and elsewhere, who might infest the hotels and ticket offices in Philadelphia and Camden where strangers about to visit Vineland stop and procure tickets. A single sample of this dishonest game will suffice :—

A stranger is seen buying a ticket for Vineland. One of these runners, while the man is waiting for the cars to start, approaches him, and, with a confidential air, inquires, " Going to Vineland ?" On receiving an affirmative answer, quietly, but with a look of ineffable scorn, he adds, " Why are you going to that God-forsaken sand-heap ? Why don't you know that the soil there is not fit even to be buried in? Have you ever been there?" "No, sir." "Well, I have, and I can assure you that they cannot even raise white beans there. For eight months in the year the mosquitoes are thick enough to eat you up, and every other man is shaking with the ague. Besides the title to the lands is not good, and if you pay your money for them you will lose both money and land. I can take you where the land is far better than it is there, and much cheaper, and where the titles are perfectly good."

The poor bewildered man says to himself, "Well, now, that is just the way some of my neighbors talked to me before I left home, and I fear there is too much truth in it," and so chagrined to think that he has come so near being cheated, or, at least, humbugged, he decides to go no further, and takes the next train of cars for home. Day after day, for the last four or five years, have these infamous wretches practised this game, sometimes inducing the unsuspecting stranger to buy of them, but oftener turning him back disgusted; and yet, through it all, and in spite of it all, Vineland has steadily grown and continues to grow.

7. Opposition to the restriction on cattle has been another serious obstacle. This opposition came from those Jerseymen who had always been in the habit of allowing their cattle to pasture in the woods and on the road-sides, and who could, with difficulty be convinced that the good of the public, and their own highest good, required the adoption of the new regulation. In fact the new regulation was at first openly defied, and the question whether it *would* be carried out, was for a time of uncertain solution. Firmness, however, on the part of Mr. Landis and his colonists was finally crowned with success, and the colony was saved from great and unnecessary expense. Since that time the same regulation has been adopted in other districts of country, and all parties have come to regard it as a wise arrangement. It is steadily growing in favor.

8. Opposition to the Liquor Law was another obstacle. Sometime after the commencement of the colony, and before restricting the sale of intoxicating drinks was passed, certain persons commenced the traffic in a quiet way, hoping, no doubt, to create a public opinion in its favor.—July 10th. 1863, an association was formed by Mr. Landis to discourage and frown down this undertaking. Strong ground was taken: both by the Proprietor and the leading colonists. A short time after a paper was circulated to test the views of the population with the following result:—For the traffic, 1: indifferent, 4: against the traffic, 227: for the traffic under certain restrictions, 1. Since then there has been no effort to establish the liquor traffic, according to law, though it has been necessary on several occasions to threaten the lawless with prosecution. On one occasion, Mr. Landis, on behalf of the Town Committee, offered a reward of fifty dollars for information that would lead to the conviction of certain persons who were supposed to be selling liquor clandestinely. This had the desired effect, and the sobriety of our colony is to-day almost without a parallel.

9. The fact that this colony was founded at a time when the people of the United States were engaged in the most gigantic war of modern times, may well be mentioned as a serious obstacle to its successful establishment. Mr. Landis made his first purchase about the time of the sad disaster at Bull Run, and began his operations at a time when the people were still in deep gloom over that defeat. For more than three years the war continued to rage, and still the course of Vineland was onward and upward. When the nation called for help, our people were not slow to respond. Our colonists have actually paid over fifty thousand dollars of direct tax for the expenses of the war, and it is with sentiments of pride that we state the fact that our people are, almost to a man, *thoroughly loyal to our government and hostile to human slavery.*

III.—*Results attained.*

Mr. Landis has purchased, at various times, lands to the amount of about twenty-eight thousand acres, or about forty-five square miles. These lands which were for the most part unimproved are located in one body in Cumberland, Gloucester, and Atlantic Counties in Southern New Jersey, in a direction nearly south from Philadelphia. The first purchase of about sixteen thousand acres, was made in 1861, the last in 1865.

Up to the present time about seventeen hundred families, numbering about eight thousand souls, have permanently located themselves on these lands, besides a floating population of about one thousand.

The various improvements effected by these people, in conjunction with the proprietor are enumerated in their order following.

FARMS, ORCHARDS, VINEYARDS AND GARDENS.

About *one thousand seven hundred and sixty farms, orchards, vineyards, and gardens* have been made in Vineland. The object of Mr. Landis was, to introduce *fruit-culture*, as a speciality, and also the highest system of farming and gardening. A good system of agriculture was required in this part of the State. The peculiar improvements which Mr. Landis has been instrumental in bringing about, in this most useful branch of industry will be found set forth in his lecture on agriculture, delivered in Vineland, in 1865. His directions have been followed with the most successful results.

It is believed that more fruit is now planted in Vineland than in any other district in America, covering the same area of land. These fruits are not poor and common varieties, but care has been taken to introduce the best varieties that could be procured. These varieties consist mainly of the following :

PEARS, (chiefly dwarf).—*Bartlett, Duchesse d'Angouleme, Louise Bonne de Jersey, Seckel, Lawrence, Sheldon, Flemish Beauty, Vicar of Wakefield, Buffum,* and some others.

APPLES. (both dwarf and standard.)—*Wagner, Northern Spy, R. Island Greening,* and other varieties most esteemed in this country.

PEACHES.—*Hale's Early, Troth's Early, Crawford's Early, Crawford's Late,* and some others.

GRAPES.—*Catawba, Concord, Delaware, Hartford Prolific, Clinton, Diana,* and some others.

STRAWBERRIES.—*Wilson's Seedling, French's Seedling, Agriculturist,* and a few others.

BLACKBERRIES.—*New Rochelle,* or *Lawton, Dorchester, Wilson,* and *Kittatinny*

RASPBERRIES.—*Doolittle's Black Cap,* and *Philadelphia.*
GOOSEBERRIES.—*Houghton's American Seedling.*
QUINCES.—*Orange* and others.
CURRANTS.—*Red Dutch, Versailles, Cherry, White Grape,* and a few others.

In riding through Vineland, the scene is of the most beautiful description, for many miles. Straight rows and clean culture are every where seen: and the cultivation and natural adaptation of the soil to fruit is such, that the trees, in their season, are loaded with delicious fruit, and the vineyards are purple with their burden of grapes. This has been brought about so suddenly as to appear almost the result of enchantment. *Five years, in this colony, have brought about results, which, almost any where else, would have absorbed the energies of an entire generation.* This fact is mainly due to the sleepless energy and singleness of purpose, with which the enterprise is conducted by Mr. Landis, and also to the facilities afforded by him to those skilled fruit-growers whom he has succeeded in attracting to Vineland.

Amongst other facilities, we will mention, that *a special agent* is employed, at the individual expense of Mr. Landis, to take charge of these fruits, when sent to market, to convert them into money, and to return the proceeds immediately to the producer. This saves the fruit-grower a great deal of time and care, and is one of the most encouraging incentives that can be given him. The *salary, travelling expenses*, and *hotel-bills* of this agent, are all paid by Mr. Landis: for which no charge is made directly or indirectly. This is done, because many of the colonists, being unacquainted in the market, would be unable to realize the full value of their products, should they attempt to market them, and would, beside the loss of valuable time, be liable to suffer from the *dishonesty* of dealers.

The *houses*, on these farms and gardens, are of the best description for such places. They are generally adorned with lattice work and creeping vines, and surrounded with flower-beds, and lawns.

Many miles of *hedges* have been planted, more for ornament than use, as cattle are not allowed to run at large. They form, however, a beautiful feature in the place. They consist of *Osage Orange, Honey Locust. Arbor Vitæ*, and *Norway Spruce.*

ROADS AND STREETS.

Besides the railroad and three other roads that were in existence in 1861, Mr. Landis has caused to be opened at his own expense forty-nine different streets and roads, measuring in the aggregate one hundred and thirty miles. On many of these roads, which traversed swamp lands, it was necessary to build up the road bed, in the soft mud at a very considerable extra expense. These roads were made through a dense wilderness of trees and undergrowth, through swamps as well as woodlands, and many of them were causeways built upon earth that had to be made solid, for a depth of many feet. Numerous bridges were also built to cross the different streams.

The following are the names and extent of the different roads, as will be found upon the map sent herewith:

Landis avenue, 3,000 rods; Elmer road, 595 rods; Sherman avenue, 871 rods; Magnolia road, 280 rods; Almond road, 315 rods; Walnut road, 1,276 rods; Myrtle street, 158 rods; Sheridan avenue, 168 rods; Orchard road, 850 rods; Fourth street, 280 rods; Elmer street, 320 rods; Quince street, 320 rods; Plum street, 320 rods; Peach street, 320 rods; Park avenue, 775 rods; Second street, 280 rods; Pear street, 320 rods; Cherry street, 320 rods; Almond street, 320 rods; Sixth street, 280 rods; Butler avenue, 600 rods; Wood street, 320 rods; Grape street, 320 rods; Eighth street, 280 rods; Valley avenue, 224 rods; Seventh street, 280 rods; Mill road, 1,530 rods; Forest Grove road, 612 rods; E. R. R. Boulevard 2,240 rods; West avenue, 1,280 rods; East avenue, 1,400 rods; Spring road, 680 rods; W. R. R. Boulevard, 2,960 rods; Montrose street, 320 rods; Third street, 280 rods; Garrison road, 240 rods; Elm road, 312 rods; Grant avenue, 505 rods; Oak road, 2,517 rods; Wheat road, 2,150 rods; Chestnut avenue, 3,000 rods; Vine road, 1,350 rods; Brewster road, 862 rods; Post road, 1,672 rods; Grove road, 1,098 rods; Garden road, 986 rods; Central road, 900 rods; Summer road, 620 rods; Union road, 720 rods.

IMPROVEMENT IN MATERIAL PROPERTY.

We regret that the limited time afforded us for making up this statement does not permit us to give anything like *full* statistics on this point, as well as on some others. We believe, however, that as many as one thousand poor people and their families have been raised from a condition of comparative poverty to one of independence; that is to say, from being in a condition in which they were compelled to work for others, in order to obtain a livelihood, by special facilities afforded them in purchasing land, making improvements, and turning their labor to profitable account, they have become possessors of lands, the cultivation of which makes them independent. The value of the different places in the

4

hands of these citizens, will range from one thousand to five thousand dollars.

It will be found, by reference to the publications of Mr. Landis, in reference to this colony, the contents of the farms offered being mostly 5, 10, and 20 acres, the purchase money payable, a small proportion in cash, and the balance by small instalments, covering a period of four years, does afford, as was intended, peculiar facilities for industrious people to purchase land. The subsequent policy of Mr. Landis being so shaped as to promote their prosperity, enables them to succeed and maintain themselves in their undertakings. The result is, that this class of people meet with complete and rapid success.

We also take this occasion to state, that notwithstanding Mr. Landis has dealt with so many thousands of different people from all countries, and of all kinds, he was never known to sue a colonist for any of his instalments, or to foreclose a mortgage. On the contrary, he has afforded this peculiar class of persons every possible facility, frequently furnishing them with lumber and other assistance, to enable them to start. We would also state, that the men who worked for him upon his roads and general improvements, he has encouraged to buy land; and, in order to enable them to do so, and get a start, he required no cash payment at all, and frequently gave them material aid besides. Almost all these men are now independent, and worth from one to two thousand dollars each.

We here take occasion to say, that these observations are not made of those wealthy people who have come in, within the past two years, and purchased places of many of the first colonists; in some cases paying *four hundred dollars* per acre, for land sold them by Mr. Landis for *twenty dollars* per acre. This great increase of price is owing to the increase of value in the property, by reason of the vast increase of population and improvements. It may be well to remark here, that the improvement stipulations of Mr. Landis extend only to the erection of a habitation, cultivating two and one-half acres of land on each place, planting shade-trees on the road-sides, and seeding the road-sides to grass. After complying with these stipulations, the colonist is at liberty to sell his property for any price that it will bring.

AGRICULTURAL IMPROVEMENTS.

In America, the waste of land by inferior cultivation is so great as to amount to a national loss. The location of Vineland near the large markets of Philadelphia and New York, afforded an opportunity to introduce the best system of farming, with the greatest profit. To the accomplishment of this object Mr. Landis bent all his energies. He wrote specific directions on the subject, which he published for the use of the colonists ; he organized Agricultural Societies ; he offered large premiums, and this aroused the interest and confidence of the people in this great work. He has been most successful in bringing about an improved system of Agriculture, as well as of Horticulture, in Vineland ; and it is believed that the example thus set will be eminently useful to all the surrounding country. We mention a few of these leading improvements, and refer, for further information, to certain publications of Mr. Landis annexed to this report.

1st. *Deep ploughing*, and *thorough harrowing*.

2d. The raising of *Root crops* for stock, as more profitable than grass.

3d. *Soiling stock*, as more profitable and *economical* than pasturing.

4th. The use of *Liquid manure*.

5th. *Underdraining*.

BEE CULTURE.

Mr. Landis has also used his best exertions for the introduction of the Bee Culture, and has succeeded to a limited

extent. Now that pasture for bees is getting plenty with
the improvements of the country, the settlers are giving it
attention. The results as yet, whilst successful so far as
produced, are not deserving of anything more than mention.
But the prospects are, that in a year or two the bee culture
will be extensive in Vineland.

DRAINING AND ITS RESULTS.

A portion of the Vineland lands, along the courses of the
streams, are *Swamp lands.* Owing to the geological formation of the Peninsula, however, these swamps are not only
free from malaria, and therefore unobjectionable on the score
of health, but they are very considerable resources of wealth.
Indeed, there *is not a drop of stagnant water naturally exist-
ing in this Colony.* All the water, even in the ponds and
marshes, is *living water,* wholesome as that of our best wells,
for drinking purposes. The swamps above referred to, have
been for ages the natural depositories for the vegetable sub-
stance called *muck* or *humus,* which, when properly treated,
proves to be a valuable *fertilizer.* Besides, portions of these
swamp-lands, where there is no muck, become, when drained,
excellent *grass-lands,* and even superior lands for the growing
of vegetables and some of the small fruits ; while the dampest
portions are all that could be desired for *Cranberry Culture.*
It is a part of Mr. Landis' plan, in conjunction with the
colonists, to drain all of these swamps, and appropriate them
to the most valuable uses. As, for obvious reasons, Mr.
Landis still owns the larger portion of these lands, he is the
owner of the larger part of the muck in the Colony. With
a liberality which proves his devotedness to the material
interests of the Colony, he has for two years past given free
permission to all the colonists to dig muck on his lands, and
has, besides, borne the principal part of the expense of drain-
ing some three hundred acres of wet land in order to enable
them to dig the muck. There are about two thousand acres
of such lands in the Colony. This system of drainage, which

is only, as it were, commenced, enables the people to dig the muck without serious hinderance.

During the winter just passed, not less that fifty thousand wagon-loads of muck have been removed from the lands of the proprietor, to the very great advantage of the colonists, many of whom are just commencing in business, and have no money with which to buy manures.

When this system of drainage shall have been completed, at least ninety-five per cent. of the wet lands in this Colony will become *arable*.

PREMIUMS

*Offered for the Encouragement of the People in Agriculture,
Horticulture, Education, &c., &c.*

In the year 1865, the Agricultural Society paid to its competing members in Premiums, an aggregate amount of nearly four hundred dollars. Of this money, Mr. Landis furnished three hundred and fifty dollars.

In the year 1866, the same Society paid an aggregate amount in similar premiums, of two hundred and twelve dollars, while the Floral Society distributed in premiums, twenty-three dollars.

In the same year, (1866,) Mr. Landis distributed the following list of premiums:

1st. One hundred dollars, to be divided in two sums, for the best essay upon the history of the place; to be determined under the supervision of the Historical Society.

2d. One hundred dollars, to be divided in two sums, for the best essay in Prose, and the best in Poetry.

One hundred dollars to the Agricultural and Horticultural Society, to be distributed as premiums for the best specimens in Produce.

One hundred dollars to the Agricultural and Horticultural Society, to be distributed as premiums for the best specimens of Fruit.

One hundred dollars, to be divided into two prize gold medals with proper inscriptions, to the two male and female scholars who shall each be pronounced the most proficient scholar, independent of any other consideration.

One hundred dollars to the two male and female scholars over fourteen years of age, and not over eighteen years of age, who shall each be pronounced the most efficient scholar, independent of any other consideration.

One hundred dollars to the Band of Music, for which they are to give six public concerts; three in the open air in summer, and three in the open air in winter.

One hundred dollars, in two gold medals, with proper inscriptions, to the two persons most graceful and proficient in gymnastics.

Fifty dollars, in a gold medal, to the lady who cultivated the best flower garden with her own hands.

Mr. Landis has also offered the following list of premiums to be distributed the present year, (1867):

Twenty dollars and certificate, for the best acre of broom corn.

Twenty dollars and certificate, for the best acre of field carrots.

Twenty dollars and certificate, for the best acre of field turnips.

Twenty dollars for the best kept farm.

Twenty dollars for the best kept orchard not less than two acres.

Fifty dollars to the lady who cultivates the best flower garden with her own hands.

One hundred dollars, to be divided between the two male and female scholars not over eighteen years of age, who shall each be pronounced the most proficient scholars.

One hundred dollars, to be divided between the three persons who are the best players on the Violin, Cornet or Bugle, and Flute; to be played at the Fair and decided by committee.

Fifty dollars to the lady most proficient in gymnastics.

Fifty dollars to the gentleman most proficient in heavy gymnastics.

The regular time for distributing all these prizes is at the Annual Fair of the Agricultural Society.

ANNUAL FAIRS.

There have been two Annual Fairs held in Vineland, the first in the fall of 1865—the other in the fall of 1866.

At these Fairs, large quantities of fruits and vegetables were exhibited, which excited the unbounded admiration of both citizens and strangers. Pears were exhibited of the variety Duchesse d'Angouleme, weighing twenty-one ounces. One exhibitor showed twelve pears of the same variety, weighing, in the aggregate, over thirteen pounds. These grew on trees that were set in the spring of the same year. One of our citizens had a dwarf pear tree of the variety Louise Bonne de Jersey, which matured one hundred and twenty-five pears.

We subjoin a copy of a photograph of this tree. It was set in its present position in the spring of 1863. We add in this connection, the fact, that at the Fair of the Farmer's Club of the American Institute, held in New York last fall, (1866,) no less than five first premiums were awarded to the Vineland exhibitors, namely, on corn, grapes, pears, (two prizes,) and for the best collection of apples, pears and quinces. Of this show, a disinterested reporter of the New York press remarked: "There are three rooms filled with fruits; a finer show of pears was never made; the Vineland pears excel."

FENCING.

By another original feature introduced by Mr. Landis, it is not required that any owner of property shall make any fence, either on the road-side or on either of his boundary lines. Should domestic animals of any kind be found running at large, they are summarily dealt with according to law. The consequence is that our streets are entirely free from the presence of these animals, and the colonists sustain no damage from their inroads, while great expense in construction and repairs of fences is saved to the people.

SHADE TREES.

By another original feature introduced by Mr. Landis, it is required that the owners of property, under a heavy penalty, shall plant shade trees along the entire front of their land at distances determined by the Township Committee. A large proportion of the shade trees planted thus far, are apple and pear trees. On the avenues one hundred feet wide, two rows of shade trees are required. Those who build houses are required to set them in the village, at least twenty

5

feet, and out of the village at least seventy-five feet from the roadside.

The object of this is to allow space in front for the cultivation of flowers and shrubbery. Already the effect is seen in an abundance of flowers rarely seen in a rural community. Not less than *one hundred miles of shade trees* have been planted along the roadsides. This is a peculiar feature, at least in the United States, introduced by Mr. Landis in the improvement of the landscape.

In America, the first propensity of a new settler is to denude the country of trees. Mr. Landis has used active and successful exertions to prevent this unfortunate propensity in Vineland. He has encouraged the settlers to leave groves of native trees remain as well as in planting. The effect of this shade tree system is the most beautiful and useful feature in Vineland. The trees shade the roads, protect the country from winds, and are believed to attract moisture. They are also friends to humanity, as their shade from the sultry heat of summer will testify. Mr. Landis has also encouraged the planting of hardy varieties of fruit trees for shade; encouraging the settlers by representing, that whilst they are doing an act profitable to their little estates, that they are also practising benevolence to all mankind and laying up blessings for posterity.

SEEDING THE ROADSIDES TO GRASS.

This feature upon so large a scale, is believed to be original with Mr. Landis. At least one hundred miles of roadsides have been seeded. In this important stipulation, the useful is attained as well as the ornamental. A large amount of land which would otherwise lay waste, is economised; weeds are usually propagated by being allowed to grow upon the roadsides from which they spread to the adjacent fields. By this arrangement this evil is effectually prevented.

INCREASE OF WAGES.

When this colony was started, (Nov. 1861,) the ruling price of wages for day laborers in this neighborhood, was fifty cents per day, cash, or seventy-five cents per day in orders upon stores; the laborer (as is the usual custom in this country,) finding himself. Mr. Landis at once put the wages up to one dollar per day in cash.

The opening of roads, building of bridges, and other preliminary improvements, gave employment to a great many poor men at these remunerative prices. A large proportion of these very men, then poor and destitute, are now the owners of comfortable homes in Vineland.

The wages for daily labor are now from $1 75 to $2 per day. This extra high price since 1861, is in part to be accounted for by the war.

MANUFACTORIES.

In the development of the elements of success in his colony, Mr. Landis recognized the important principle that home manufacture should be started and encouraged, in order to economise the wealth, the labor, and the skill of the colonists.

For this purpose he encouraged the erection of steam mills for the manufacturing of rough lumber into building material,—doors, sashes, blinds, lath, shingles and flooring; also turning establishments for ornamental work.

In order to attain these results speedily and effectually, Mr. Landis, in the winter of 1864 and 1865, erected large buildings with steam power. This was done to accommodate industrious and useful but poor mechanics, who might not have the means to erect large works and buy engines, but who had tools with which to carry on their business by renting rooms and power. These buildings were erected at a cost of $27,000. They are now occupied by a machinist, a grist and flouring mill, a wood turning establishment and fruit canning company, for the canning of small fruits and the manufacture of tin cans. A manufactory for making clothing has been introduced, and the machinery is in the building, but it has not yet started. It is expected that this season various other mechanical branches of manufacturing will be introduced into these buildings.

For these purposes five other steam mills have been also erected by private individuals. Mr. Landis, in co-operation with other citizens, organized a fruit canning establishment, called

The Vineland Canning and Fruit-Preserving Company.

Organized April 3, 1866; recently incorporated by special act of the Legislature. Objects.—To preserve all kinds of fruits and vegetables that can be canned successfully, especially to use up those productions, which at certain seasons of the year cannot be profitably disposed of in the cities, and to afford employment, at good wages, to women and children who may need such employment.

The capital stock of this company at present amounts to $9,675,—number of stockholders, 147; between two-fifths and three-fifths of whom are comparatively poor. The number of cans of fruit put up last year, in gallons, 1,400; others, smaller, 60,000, with the exception of peaches, nearly all of this fruit was grown in Vineland.

Also, a manufactory of palm leaf into shaker hood bonnets, called

The Vineland Palm Leaf and Shaker Hood Manufacturing Company.

Recently incorporated by special act of the Legislature.

This company gives employment directly and indirectly, to about 300 people. The palm leaf is cut into strips and then woven into webs. This latter part of the work is done in the houses of the citizens, by girls, boys, and housewives, in their spare moments.

The capital stock of this company is now $6,537 45. Number of stockholders, 200; at least two-thirds of whom are comparatively poor, (very many of the stockholders work for the company). Women and children employed in weaving and other work, 310, who can, on an average, earn from 50 cents to $1 00 per day. Number of hands employed in shop.—males, 12; females, 8. Average wages of males, $1 64 per day; of females, $1 05 per day. Value of goods manufactured the past year, about $10,000.

Four Brick Yards are carried on in the summer time, for the manufacture of our clay into bricks.

A manufactory for the making of stone-ware pottery out of our clay. This is now successfully carried on, and promises to become very extensive.

The small establishments of shoemakers, weavers, tailors and others being strictly private and individual, are not mentioned.

SOCIETIES OF VARIOUS KINDS.

1.—*The Philanthropic Loan Association.*

This is an association of a benevolent character, organized October 11th, 1865, with a membership of about TWO HUNDRED. It was originated by Mr. Landis, and is one of the peculiar institutions of our colony. So far as we know, there is nothing similar to it elsewhere. It is patronized by all the more wealthy of our citizens. Its object is to loan money to the necessitous, solely upon the honor of the borrower, without interest, to be paid back as soon as convenient. It is distinctly understood that the borrower is not to take advantage of this circumstance, but shall return the money as soon as he possibly can. The reasons for the formation of such an association are the following:—Some people, in the enthusiasm attendant upon the making of new improvements, neglect to cultivate sufficient land the first season for the support of their families; others imprudently or injudiciously expend their labor or means. In either case, when winter comes, many such families find themselves in straightened circumstances. They are, however, entirely too proud to ask charity, and would not accept it unless forced to it by biting want. Some would even be unwilling to have their condition known to their neighbors, nor would such be willing to accept a loan on the ordinary condition of repaying the money at a certain definite time; their income being too precarious for the time being to assure the ability to pay at any definite time. This association, therefore, loans them the money on the terms above-mentioned, with the strict understanding that it is a *loan*, and not a *gift*, and that payment will be expected at some time or other, and to the honor of humanity we are glad to state that thus far but little, if any, of the money thus loaned has been lost. The *benevolence* of this association is the more clearly seen from the fact that since the date of its organization, and even before that time, money in this country has commanded a very high rate of interest—*ten per cent.*, being the lowest rate at which most persons can borrow it.

Up to the present time, this association has assisted nearly fifty persons with loans, running from one to twelve months, the whole amounting to nearly *eight hundred dollars.* This money was procured by loans and contributions from citizens, rich and poor, who are members of the association; also, by giving balls, concerts and dramatic entertainments for the benefit of the society.

The Vineland Historical and Antiquarian Society.

Organized February 3d, 1864. Number of Members 30—Objects.—To collect and preserve interesting relics and minerals, also documents, especially relating to Vineland, and to procure lectures for the people on important and interesting subjects.

The Vineland Pioneer Association.

Organized December 12th, 1866. Members limited to those who were residents of Vineland, prior to January 1st,

1863. Objects.—To celebrate the Anniversary of the close of the first year in Vineland. Meets annually on the evening of December 31st. Present number of members 75.

Vineland Lodge, No. 69, A. F. and A. M.

Number of members, 70.—Meets in Vineland semi-monthly.

Loyal League.

Number of members, about 325. This is a secret political organization, the object of which is to perpetuate liberty and free institutions on the Americrn continent.—Meets weekly.

Liberty Lodge, No. 1.—Good Templars.

A secret temperance organization: organized July 21st, 1866. Objects.—To promote the cause of temperance throughout our land; to raise the fallen and to keep others from ever falling into the snares of the tempter.

Number of members, 93: degree members, 25.— Meets in Vineland Weekly.

Young People's Union Christian Association.

Organized March 13th, 1866. Number of members, 80. Objects.—To promote the social, moral and religious improvement of all its members: and to work zealously and untiringly for the social welfare and salvation of all. This association holds weekly meetings. It likewise sustains some six Sunday Schools in the more remote parts of the colony.

The People's Lyceum.

Number of members, 137. Objects.—To hear declamations and original compositions and orations from members; to debate questions proposed, and to secure the literary advancement of the members.—Meets weekly in Vineland.

The Vineland Library Association.

Organized January, 1867. Number of members, about 150. Objects.—To establish and maintain a library for the use of its members, to hold meetings for discussion, to procure public lectures, to make historical and other collections, and, in general, to advance the members in literature, science and art. Number of volumes in the library, over 500.

Music.

The cultivation of music was a subject among the first to receive the attention of Mr. Landis. In 1862 he formed a band of seven instruments, and since then by contributing money, offering premiums, and other methods he has been directly or indirectly instrumental in the formation of the following societies.

The Harmonic Association.

Objects.—To promote the theory and practice of vocal and instrumental music, especially the former, and to give public rehearsals and concerts.

Societies for the Promotion of Agriculture, Horticulture and Flowers.

We can do little more than give a list of these societies.

The Vineland Agricultural and Horticultural Society.

Objects.—To promote the interests of agriculture and horticulture, to discuss all questions pertaining to the same, and to hold fairs and exhibitions of agricultural and horticultural products, to encourage industry, by offering suitable prizes, and to increase the knowledge of the people by lectures, periodicals. &c.

Organized June 2, 1863. Number of members at the present time, 350.

Meets weekly in Vineland.

The Vineland Floral Society.

This was a society organized by Mr. Landis, among the ladies of Vineland, for the purpose of encouraging the cultivation of flowers and out-door physical exercise.

The ladies of Vineland have taken an enthusiastic interest in the subject, and it has been attended with the happiest results. Bulbs, roots and seeds have been gratuitously distributed over the settlement, so thoroughly and successfully that the humblest cottages are surrounded with flowers and shrubbery. Premiums have been offered by Mr. Landis for the best gardens of flowers cultivated by the hands of the ladies, and not by gentlemen, and the result has been not only to produce a great number of beautiful flowers, but to make out-door exercise, in the cultivation of flowers, fashionable in Vineland, no matter what their wealth or social position. Many ladies who were confirmed invalids have been entirely cured by this out-door exercise.

South Vineland Fruit Growers' Club.

Objects.—To promote the interests of Horticulture and Agriculture, and to discuss all questions relating to Manures, Crops, Markets, &c. Connected with this Club is a Library of 200 volumes.

East Vineland Agricultural and Pomological Society.

Objects as indicated by its title. Organized September 21, 1866. Number of Members, 25. Meets weekly at East Vineland.

Forest Grove Horticultural and Agricultural Society.

Number of Members, 35.
Object as indicated by its title. Meets in North Vineland weekly.

Hamilton Mutual Benefit Society.

Organized November 22, 1866. Number of Members, 25. Object similar to those above described.

The Philathletic Club.

Number of Members, 20. Object. To promote a knowledge of the laws of health, and to train the members in athletic exercises.

6

The Vineland Loan and Improvement Association.

Recently incorporated by Special Act of the Legislature. Number of Members, 50. Objects. To afford facilities of investment of small sums to the laboring classes and small capitalists, and to loan money to its members, on easy terms of monthly payments. Meets in Vineland, on the first Tuesday in each month.

Siloam Cemetery Association.

An incorporated Society. The Cemetery grounds comprise nearly 15 acres, 10 of which were donated by Mr. Landis and are partially improved.

We enclose a copy of the Plan of the Cemetery, adopted by the Trustees. Already, over $1,500 have been expended in beautifying the grounds.

CHURCH ORGANIZATIONS.

The Protestant Episcopal Church (Trinity.)

Organized August 19, 1863. Number of Communicants. 73. Average attendance, 200.
Sunday School Teachers, 7. Scholars. 60.

First Presbyterian Church.

Organized June 4. 1863. Number of Members, 270. Average attendance, about 350.
Sunday School Teachers. 33. Scholars, 200.

First Methodist Episcopal Church.

Organized April 12. 1863. Number of Members, 200. Average attendance, 400.
Sunday School Teachers. 22. Scholars. 150.

First Baptist Church.

Organized June 13, 1865. Number of Members. 100. Average attendance. about 200.

Sunday School Teachers, 17.   Scholars, 160.
Number of volumes in Library, 300.

Unitarian Church.

Organized April 5, 1866.   Number of Members, 250; representing about 250 families.

There is a Sunday School connected with this Church.

Free Will Baptist Church of South Vineland.

Organized recently.   Number of Members, 18.

"Friends of Progress."

Organized July 3d, 1864.   Number of Members, 175. Average attendance, 175.   Sunday School (Children's Lyceum) about 75.   Weekly Sociable—average attendance about 300.

Besides the foregoing, the Methodist Church has a branch that holds meetings at their Church, at South Vineland. Meetings are also held in several School-houses on Sundays. In almost every neighborhood there are meetings for prayer and conference, held in private houses, on stated evenings during the week.

The Catholic Church

Has been offered a donation of lots by Mr. Landis, but they have not yet effected an organization.   This is expected to take place in the spring of this year.

POST OFFICES.

Since the formation of the Colony there have been *three* post-offices established upon this tract of land—one at Vineland, one at North Vineland, and one at South Vineland, with a daily mail to and from, of about 600 letters.

The Vineland Post-office is one of the few post-offices in Southern New Jersey through which the General Government transmits funds by the system of "*Money Orders*."

The revenue of this office, for the year 1866, amounted to $5,991 $\frac{39}{100}$.

NEWSPAPERS.

There are now three newspapers published in Vineland.

"The Vineland Rural," has been published ever since the first year of the Colony. It is filled with Agricultural matter, descriptions of Vineland, reports of its progress, evidences as to the fertility of its soil, its capabilities, &c. It is distributed in large numbers *gratuitously*, and is mainly intended as an *advertising medium*.

"The Vineland Weekly," which is a first-class weekly family newspaper, was first issued Sept. 9, 1865. It has a circulation of about fifteen hundred, and has been enlarged since its commencement. It publishes Reports of the Agricultural and other Societies, all the various Local Items, selections of reading matter, Foreign and Domestic News, and, besides, regular weekly correspondence from Washington and Trenton.

"The Vineland Independent," the other weekly paper, has but just started. We can, therefore, give no further information in regard to it.

A Job Printing Office is connected with each of these weekly papers.

PUBLIC BUILDINGS.

The Presbyterian Church.—Frame building, with slate roof; weight of bell, 2,000 lbs.; entire cost, about $8,000. The edifice is already too small to accommodate the congregation, and steps are being taken for its enlargement.

The Protestant Episcopal Church.—Frame building, with steeple, and bell weighing 800 lbs.

Plum Street Hall.—This building is the meeting-place of the "Friends of Progress." It is one story high, cost about $4,000.

The Methodist Episcopal Church.—Stone and brick, two stories, slate roof, unfinished, but now in process of erection. Estimated cost, about $14,000. This will be a beautiful structure when completed.

The Congregational Church, at North Vineland.—A frame building, with steeple.

The Methodist Episcopal Church, in South Vineland.—Frame building, one story.

Besides the above described Churches, the *Baptist Society* have made arrangements for erecting, the coming summer, a church building, at an estimated cost of at least seven thousand dollars ; the larger portion of the funds, for this purpose, have already been subscribed and the lots purchased.

The Unitarian Society have also commenced a church building, of stone and brick, two stories high, 45 by 80 feet, which will be erected during the coming summer.

The Free-Will Baptists, of South Vineland, are also about building a church there.

SCHOOL-HOUSES.

Young Ladies' and Gentlemen's Academy.—This is a building erected by Mr. Landis. Object. To instruct pupils in the higher elements of an English, French and Latin education. Three Teachers are employed. Several scholars in this Academy have won different prizes offered by Mr. Landis for proficiency in scholarship.

Besides this Academy, since the commencement of this Colony, there have been erected within its bounds *thirteen School-Houses*, (two of which are of brick,) at an aggregate cost of fifteen thousand dollars.

We append a list of some of the more important buildings, more or less public in their character.

Factory Buildings, with Steam Power.—Erected by Mr. Landis, in order to enable manufacturers to rent Room and Power, occupied for various manufacturing purposes.

Flouring-Mill, Wood-Turning, &c.—One of the buildings is designed for a Foundry. Cost of the whole, about $27,000.

Mechanics Hall, of brick, three stories high, with a basement, occupied for Stores. Offices and a Public Hall. Cost about $9,000.

Paine & Mabbett's Sash. Door and Blind Factory, with Steam Power.

Tomkins & Gay's Planing-Mill, with Steam Power.

Railroad Depot.--Stone building, with Hall on second floor.

Temperance Hall.--Frame, two stories, with basement. Hall on second floor.

Masonic Hall.--Frame, two stories. Hall on second floor.

Maynolia Hotel.--Frame, three stories high. Cost about ten thousand dollars.

Besides those enumerated, there are numerous Store Buildings, and Mechanics' Shops, costing from one thousand to five thousand dollars each.

SIGNERS TO THE FOREGOING STATEMENT.

Signed,

F. C. B. CHUBBUCK,
Rector of Trinity Church, (Protestant Episcopal)
Vineland, N. J.

" ROBERT J. ANDREWS,
Pastor of First Methodist Episcopal Church,
Vineland, N. J.

" J. O. WELLS,
Pastor of First Presbyterian Church,
Vineland, N. J.

" J. C. PARSONS,
President Historical Society,
Vineland, N. J.

" M. C. CROCKER,
President of Library Association,
Vineland, N. J.

" PHILIP SNYDER,
President Vineland Agricultural and
Horticultural Society.

" C. B. CAMPBELL,
President of Friends of Progress,
Vineland, N. J.

" CHAS. K. LANDIS, *Chairman,* ⎫
" GEO. W. COTTRELL,   TOWNSHIP COMMITTEE
" GEORGE PEARSON,   OF LANDIS TOWNSHIP,
" JOHN C. WHEELER,   NEW JERSEY.
" HAZEN Z. ELLIS, ⎭

Signed,

"   WILLIAM O. H. GWYNNETH,

Town Clerk, Landis Township.

"   JOHN KANDLE,

Chosen County Freeholder.

"   JAMES H. NIXON,

Member of the Legislature of New Jersey, from the
Twenty-second District of Cumberland County,
embracing Vineland.

"   REV. MARTIN GESSNER,

Pastor of the Catholic Church in Millville, the
nearest to Vineland.

"   THEO. G. COMPTON,

County Clerk of the County of Cumberland.

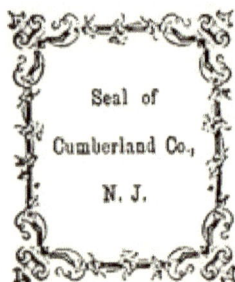

Seal of
Cumberland Co.,
N. J.

WITNESS my hand and seal of the County, this
eleventh day of March, one thousand eight
hundred and sixty-seven, (1867.)

"   JOSEPH W. MORTON,

President of Siloam Cemetery Association.

"   PROVIDENCE LUDLAM,

Senator from Cumberland County,

New Jersey.

EXECUTIVE CHAMBER.

To the International Jury of the Paris Exhibition:

THIS IS TO CERTIFY, That Charles K. Landis is the Founder of the Colony of Vineland, in New Jersey: that he is a gentleman of character, culture and ability, and that his statements may be relied on for truth and correctness.

This is further to Certify, That the names appended to the foregoing statements are genuine, and that the persons are what they represent themselves to be.

In Testimony Whereof, I have hereunto set my hand and caused the great seal of the State to be affixed at Trenton.

WITNESS, Marcus L. Ward, Governor of the State of New Jersey, this thirteenth day of March, A. D. eighteen hundred and sixty-seven, and of the Independence of the United States the ninety-first.

By the Governor,

(Signed,)   MARCUS L. WARD.